D1337978

*Some light reading
for the holiday break!*

The feckin' book
of Bankers, Builders,
Blaggers and
Bowsies that
banjaxed the nation

The Feckin' Collection

COLIN MURPHY and DONAL O'DEA are the co-authors of fourteen hugely successful Feckin' books which deal with yokes as diverse as Irish Slang, Sex, History, Insults and Trivia, to mention but a few. Their latest collaboration takes a gander at the unholy shenanigans of all the blundering bankers, builders, biffos and other bowsies, ourselves included, who made a hames of the country.

COLIN MURPHY is considered an expert in the field of debt, as, like Ireland, he is utterly broke and, due to his excessive drinking habits, currently owes more money than he can ever repay in his lifetime. He is married to Grainne and has two teenage offspring who have adopted Irish property developers as their role models, i.e. they spend money like it's going out of fashion.

DONAL O'DEA is widely regarded as someone who has a deep empathy with our current banking system, as, like the banks, he is as tight as a camel's arse in a sandstorm. He is married to Karen and has three young children whose combined knowledge of basic economics vastly exceeds that of the entire Department of Finance.

First published 2010 by The O'Brien Press Ltd,
12 Terenure Road East, Rathgar, Dublin 6, Ireland.
Tel: +353 1 4923333; Fax: +353 1 4922777
E-mail: books@obrien.ie; Website: www.obrien.ie

ISBN: 978-1-84717-241-9

A catalogue record for this title is available from the British Library

1 2 3 4 5 6 7 8 9 10
10 11 12 13

Printed and bound by Scandbook AB, Sweden.
The paper in this book is produced using pulp from managed forests.

The feckin' book of Bankers, Builders, Blaggers and Bowsies that banjaxed the nation

Colin Murphy & Donal O'Dea

THE O'BRIEN PRESS
DUBLIN

What the feck?

'Going forward in the past, our horizon scanning indicated that light touch regulation and cross fertilisation would provide more bang for our buck. At this juncture however, the prevailing philosophy is that we are where we are, and we believe that focusing on customer-centric decisioning will boost the country's income stream and produce the first green shoots.'

You've probably heard this sort of oul' bullshit a hundred times these past few years but what in feck's name does it mean?

By the time you get to the end of this book, it will make perfect sense, i.e. you'll realise that the bankers and their political cronies and all the rest of the gougers who got us into this mess were talking through their arses all along!

Affluenza

Disease affecting Irish people who spent money like mad bowsies during the 'boom' and now have to flog off their 4-wheel drives and holiday homes so they can afford a jacks roll. Symptoms include whingeing and secretly shopping in cheap foreign supermarkets.

Allied Irish Bank

Up to a couple of years ago AIB would lend any amount of money to any eejit like there was no tomorrow. And guess what? There wasn't. Now they're so banjaxed that if you go to inquire about a loan, the first thing they ask is how much you can afford to lend them.

Anacronym

A fusion of anachronism and acronym, ie acronyms that belong to a long gone era. Examples:

DINKY *(Dual Income No Kids Yet)* – These have now become SINKYS or NINKYS. *(Single Income or No Income)*

TGIF *(Thank God It's Friday)* – No one has the dosh to go on the batter at the weekend anymore.

WOOPIE *(Well-Off Older Person)* – Lost all their money investing in shares.

WAAAH!!! I DON'T WANT A LOLLIPOP. I WANT AN iPHON WAAAH!!!

THE NOW OBSOLETE 'SKIPPY' (SCHOOL KID WITH PURCHASING POWER)

Anglo Irish Bank

Now owned by the taxpayer, this 'bank' was once managed by a collection of greedy gougers the likes of which is rarely seen outside of gangland. These chancers are a walking argument for contraception.

MY LAWYER IS TRYING TO RE-REGISTER MY NEW YORK BANK AS AN IRISH BANK. THAT WAY I'LL NOT ONLY GET OFF SCOTT FREE, BUT I'LL BE RE-APPOINTED TO THE BOARD.

Artists Exemption

Formerly a tax break to help poor artists to survive, now a tax break to help ex-Taoisigh who've written their memoirs to put the boot into taxpayers while they're on their knees. Put the country first? I will in me arse.

At This Juncture

Jargon that supposedly means 'yet', but actually means 'not a snowball's chance in hell of it ever happening'. For example: 'No formal charges have been brought against banking officials at this juncture' means, 'Arrest our bosom buddies in the banking sector? In your dreams, suckers!'

ATM

Machine that saves you the pain in the bollix of having to deal with a banker face to face.

Auditor

An 'expert' who makes sure that all those plus and minus columns that don't mean head or tail to the company director read like a beautiful symphony that makes sweet music to the ears of the taxman.

Bailout

Free money given away by a government to pay back pals in the banking sector. In order to qualify for a bailout you must:

1) Have demonstrated your complete inability to be put in charge of running anything larger than a vegetable stall in Moore Street.

2) Be completely devoid of business ethics.

3) Lay on lavish meals for political allies in Dublin's finest restaurants.

Bang For Your Buck

What your money will buy you. Generally goes up during a recession when all the boyos who ripped us off during the boom come crawling to us begging for a

morsel of business. Ah… revenge
is a dish best served cold!

Bank Manager

Once a pillar of the community, the
position of bank manager now
ranks somewhere between that of
a dodgy secondhand car salesman
and Imelda Marcos.

Bankroll

To finance. Virtually obsolete, as many people can barely afford to bankroll an evening on the batter.

Bear Market

When the stock market is banjaxed for yonks, e.g. when your bank shares go from being worth €20 each to being worth the same as a floozie's pair of ten-year-old knickers, and have about the same chance of improving in value.

Benchmarking

Redundant term used by the Government to buy votes by giving the public service gansey-loads of money for doing nothing in particular.

Bertienomics
(see also Benchmarking/ Artists Exemption)

Economic strategy designed to keep Fianna Fáil in power no matter how much it banjaxes the country in the long term. Revolves around the principle of giving tax breaks to sleeveens, not keeping a personal bank account and going to watch Manchester United with cronies.

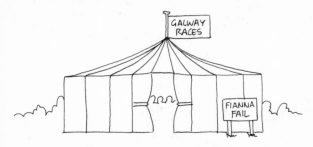

GALWAY RACES

FIANNA FAIL

THE IRISH INSTITUTE OF BERTIENOMICS

Best Practice

The optimum method of ignoring regulations, planning, tax law, business ethics etc in order to screw one's customers, shareholders and the taxpayer and make oneself loads of dosh.

Blue Sky Thinking

Cringe-inducing oul' blather for thinking that is unburdened by negativity.

B.o.I.

Bowsies of Ireland, as it is more widely known, was the scene of one of the largest daylight bank robberies in the history of the state when a bunch of gougers entered the bank's headquarters in College Green and were handed billions by the bankers to invest in worthless property deals so they could all get rich. And they got clean away with it.

Bonus

Ginormous amount of money given to cute hoors who are in the know. Usually awarded for bankrupting a company or fiddling expenses from the state.

Bottom Line

The true measure of just how financially banjaxed you are!

Bottom up approach

Working from the basics of a problem to formulate a successful outcome to the task in hand. See diagram below.

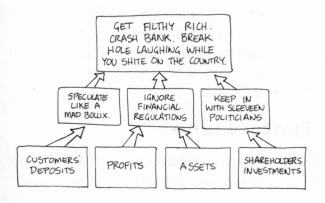

Budget Deficit

About 50 Billion Euro.

Capital Injection

An amount of taxpayers' money handed to a bunch of reckless gobshites to keep their company afloat, granted particularly in circumstances where the company directors are as useful as a one-armed man climbing a rope.

CEO

The Chief Embezzlement Officer.

'Bank of Ireland shares are €3.80 today. Now if I meet you here next year, or the year after, do you seriously think Bank of Ireland shares will be €3.80? I'd go out and buy Bank of Ireland shares ... that's what I'd do.'

Former Taoiseach Bertie Ahern,
The Irish Times *19 September 2008.*

On 11 March 2009 BOI shares were worth 22cent.

Core Competencies

A central factor that defines what a business or institution is good at. For example, a core competency of some of Ireland's county councils is granting planning permission for housing estates slap bang in the middle of flood plains.

Cost Reduction Initiative

Firing a bunch of ordinary Joe Soaps to save money because you've made a right hames of running the business and want to keep your yacht and villas in Italy.

BULLSHIT BOX

'If we try to shackle entrepreneurs instead of encouraging them, the country is going to suffer. Part of the shackling is the huge emphasis on regulation and that can't be good for business.'

Sean Fitzpatrick, former Chairman of Anglo Irish Bank, in a Times *profile, December 2008.*

Coughlanism

A term used to describe someone putting their foot in their mouth. Example: 'Of the savings of €100 million, €86 million is for GPs and €30 million is for pharmacists.' – *Mary Coughlan speaking in the Dáil on the medical card row in 2008.* Or:
'The IDA would be marketing Ireland as the innovation island, like Einstein explaining his theory

of evolution.' – *Coughlan again, speaking at an IDA 'Innovation Ireland' launch in September 2009.*

Credit Crunch

The banks refusing to lend money to businesses, despite the fact that the geebags have been bailed out by the taxpayer.

TALK ABOUT CREDIT CRUNCH... I LENT MICK €50 IN THE PUB LAST WEEK AND I'VE JUST DISCOVERED I'M IRELAND'S FOURTH BIGGEST LENDER.

BULLSHIT BOX

'However, what we do know is that the underlying demand for housing remains strong, driven by a relatively young population and continued inward migration. While we may experience a year or two of sub-50,000 completions, it is reasonable to expect over the medium term that annual comple- tions will return to sustainable levels which will remain high by international standards, reflecting the strong underlying demand for housing in Ireland.'

Brian Lenihan, Minister for Finance, in a Seanad Éireann speech, 14 May 2008.

Credit Rating Agency

A company that tells you how much of a risk you are to lend money to. Currently, Ireland's risk status is roughly equivalent to a man soaking his clothes in petrol while trying to put out a fire by beating down the flames with a box of fireworks.

Cross Fertilisation

An exchange of knowledge or expertise between diverse groups that will be mutually beneficial to both. For example, when a gombeen man from a state agency gets a promotion from a cute hoor politician in exchange for ideas about fiddling his/her expenses.

Currency Crisis

When the value of a currency changes so quickly that, as a medium of exchange, it is about as useless as a concrete currach.

Customer Centric

When a company puts the needs of its customers first, as opposed to working like the clappers to screw their customers for every cent they can.

Cutbacks

Taking money from the poor to bail out the rich feckers who banjaxed the country in the first place.

CYA

Expression meaning to 'cover your arse', or to make sure you've hidden any dodgy dealings from your boss, the taxman, the public, the Gardaí, your conscience etc.

Decruitment

Giving temporary/trainee/intern workers the bleedin' boot before they've even been offered a proper job.

BULLSHIT BOX

'In recent months an acceleration in Irish house price inflation has raised concerns that the property market might be developing in a way that threatens not only the stability of that market but also the health of the broader Irish economy. I think these fears are exaggerated.'

Austin Hughes, Chief Economist, IIB Bank, addressing the Irish Home Builders Association, 12 May 2008.

Debt Speculation

This involves two Fianna Fáil TDs having a pint as they speculate on how in the name of Jaysus they'll be re-elected considering the debt their policies have put the country in.

Decisioning

Idiotic business jargon for 'making decisions'. Anyone who uses this to you can be earmarked for future reference as a dim-witted gobshite.

Developer

The property developer was once viewed, particularly by politicians and bankers, as the Master Of The Known Universe and the God Before Whom All Must Bow and Lick Arse. As the properties that some of them developed for bilions are now worth less than a weightlifter's old jockstrap, the self-same developers are now viewed as The Shower of Savages Who Helped Make A Hames of The Country.

AND THE 3 LEAVES
REPRESENT THE BANKERS,
THE DEVELOPERS
AND FIANNA FÁIL...

USING THE SHAMROCK, ST. PATRICK EXPLAINS
THE MYSTERY OF THE UNHOLY TRINITY

Disambiguate

Unintentionally ironic jargon
meaning 'to clarify'. The product of
a sick mind.

Double-Dip Recession

When an economy recovers after a
quarter or two and then nosedives
again. This term does not apply to
Ireland, where our economy has

been classified as 'The Downward-Spiral-Into-Oblivion Recession.'

Downsizing

Term used by company bosses who are trying to find a nice way to tell their staff that they are being kicked out of the company on their arses.

SPEAKING PLAINLY MISS KELLY, AS PART OF OUR OVERHEAD RETROSPECTION AUDIT, OUR PERSONNEL RE-ALIGNMENT DETERMINATOR HAS SELECTED YOU FOR OUR DOWNSIZING INITIATIVE.

SPEAKING JUST AS PLAINLY MR RICE, YE CAN SHOVE YER JOB UP YER ARSE YE BALDY LITTLE BOLLIX!

Downturn

What happens to the faces of Irish solicitors when a tribunal finishes.

Due Diligence

In other countries they had 'due diligence' i.e. the care and attention paid to the details of a transaction before a deal is done. In Ireland during the 'boom' we had 'due negligence'.

BULLSHIT BOX

'The government guarantee of Irish banks had ensured "the cheapest bailout in the world so far".'

Minister for Finance, Brian Lenihan, as reported in The Irish Times, *October 2008.*

Expenses

Money paid to TDs and senior public servants (and spouses) for sunning their arses by the poolsides of 5-star hotels etc while they snigger at us for being such gobshites in keeping them in their jobs.

HEY MICK, ARE YOU SURE WE CAN COVER THESE GIRLS ON EXPENSES?

DEFFO. CLAIM IT UNDER 'SCREWING THE TAXPAYER'

Face Time

Bullshit for 'having a meeting'. Alternative meanings are: doing your make-up, or snogging the face off some youngwan or youngfella.

SORRY I'M LATE DARLING. HAD TO GIVE SOME FACETIME TO MISS KELLY.

Fianna Fáil

Former political party. The second half of their name should be pronounced as though it was an English word.

Financial Meltdown

A financial crisis triggered by the gross overvaluation of various things, mainly the ethics and intelligence of bankers, developers, ministers and senior political advisers.

MINISTER! IT'S A FINANCIAL MELTDOWN! WE'VE BANKRUPTED THE COUNTRY! COUNTLESS JOB LOSSES AND ALL THE MONEY WE SQUANDERED!

RELAX! SURE WE CAN JUST SLASH THE OLD AGE PENSION!

Financial Regulator

Well, didn't we all think that our political masters and the geniuses in the Dept of Finance were on the ball with the creation of the post of Financial Regulator? It would be something like having a regulator on your electricity supply to make sure you didn't overload the national grid every time you turned on the oven - wouldn't it?

We were wrong! It turned out that the regulation was to be done with a lighter touch than that required for making puff pastry, and, when the bubble finally burst we discovered that our finances were about as regulated as Colombian soccer supporters who've been denied a crucial victory by a bad refereeing decision.

Finger of Blame

Unfortunately, we don't have enough fingers to point at all the eejits who contributed to the recession, which includes half the population.

I POINT THE FINGER OF BLAME AT THE BANKS. FOR JAYSUS SAKE, THEY LENT ME ENOUGH TO BUY THREE APARTMENTS IN DUBAI, A JACUZZI IN MY BEDROOM, MY DAUGHTER'S HUMMER, AND TO PAY FOR A SPACE FLIGHT ON SOYUZ 15 AND I ONLY EARN €30K A YEAR.

THE BASTARDS!

BULLSHIT BOX

'But there is no place for negativity. No need for any pessimism. Above all, there is no place for politically motivated attempts to talk down the economy and the achievements of our people across all sectors.'

Former Taoiseach Bertie Ahern
Fianna Fáil website, September 2007.

Fiscal Adjustment

Fancy bullshit for slashing spending and hoofing up taxes after you've made such a hames of the economy that the budget deficit is as sick as a plane to Lourdes.

Funemployment

Unemployment is great! You have all that time to spend frolicking through fields of daisies in your threadbare clothes. Can't afford to feed the family? Don't be so negative! Simply go on a fun diet this month! Can't pay the electric bill? You're helping the environment by not wasting energy with stupid oul' radiators. House repossessed? Hey kids … how about we all go camping in a field? See? The executive sleeveens who coined the term 'funemployment' were right all along!

YEAH IT'S OKAY. — I'M FUNEMPLOYED.

G.D.P.

Originally stood for Gross Domestic Product, which is basically the country's economic output. As ours is currently about the same as Botswana's, it now stands for Growth-Defying Poverty.

Ghost Estates

'If you build it, they will come', so went the famous line from the movie 'Field of Dreams'. This was the thinking behind the building during the boom of countless thousands of houses we didn't need, resulting in virtually vacant 'Ghost Estates' (term coined by David McWilliams) all over the country. Our landscape will be haunted by these crumbling monstrosities for decades.

Giz a Job

A term made famous during the recession in the 1980s, now sadly enjoying a revival. If there is an up side, remember how you couldn't get a tradesman of any description during the boom without having to beg, wait two months and then take out a second mortgage just to have an extra socket fitted or a window latch fixed? Nowadays it's 'giz a job, missus'.

Going Forward

Taoiseach's Adviser: See, instead of saying 'In de future', if you say 'Going forward', it makes you sound more pro-active, like you're actually doing something.

Taoiseach: Yeah… yeah… I can see that… I'll tell you what, I'll use it in every second sentence, then I'll sound really pro-active.

Taoiseach's Adviser: (To himself) Or you could sound like an ignorant mucksavage who doesn't know his arse from his elbow.

BULLSHIT BOX

'I reject the suggestion that banks have been foolhardy in recklessly lending and driving up values… I cannot think of a bank that has been reckless.'

Willie McAteer, former Executive Director at Anglo Irish Bank, speaking in July 2008.

Golden Circle

A shady shower of gougers at the top of Irish business and public life who scratch each other's backs so they can keep their grimy little fingers on their millions. Allegedly, the 'Golden Circle' regularly meet in secret to hold Satanic rituals, indulge in outrageous gluttony and perverted orgies, dress in ladies underwear and flog each other for pleasure.

No? Any member of the 'Golden Circle' who wishes to go public and contradict this description, please be our guest.

WEAR THIS GOLDEN CIRCLE YOUNG SEAN, AND IT WILL FOREVER MAKE YOU INVISIBLE TO REGULATORY BODIES, THE TAXMAN AND THE GARDAI.

Governance

The act of governing: Health
service banjaxed. Banking systems
arseways. Prison system a hames.
Water supply wrecked. Gammy
public transport. 'Planning' a
a wojus free-for all, etc., etc.,
etc. All this despite a decade of
record tax takes. That's gover-
nance, Irish style!

Great Depression

What estate agents are likely to feel for a long time to come.

Greece

Instead of wasting taxpayers' money sending councillors on junkets to 'twin' with other little arse-end-of-nowhere towns in Europe, we should just twin the whole country with Greece.

Green Shoots

The first signs of recovery. Fianna Fáil politicians have been seeing them everywhere for nearly two years now. These mythical green shoots thrive in desolate, unproductive land and need constant supplies of bullshit or they keep withering.

BULLSHIT BOX

'Every loan goes through a central credit committee and is properly underwritten.'

Willie McAteer, former Executive Director of Anglo Irish Bank, to the Oireachtas Finance Committee, 2 July 2008.

Hedge Fund

Hedge funds are supposed to be 'hedged' from risk, hence the name. They use a broad range of generally high-risk (dodgy?) investments, including shares, debt and commodities. They are not subject to regulation, so they're particularly loved in Ireland, where rich people get annoyed by those gammy oul' rules and regulations. The Department of Finance only recently discovered that Hedge Funds did not mean investing in a Garden Centre.

Horizon Scanning

Wojus jargon for trying to predict the financial future.

THAT HORIZON SCANNING YOU ASKED FOR? I'M AFRAID IRELAND HAS SUNK WITHOUT A TRACE...

Iceland

Relative to its economy, Iceland had the biggest banking collapse in world history. There is no truth to the rumour that they were being advised by Ireland's Department of Finance.

WHERE'S ALL THE ASH COMING FROM?

ICELAND'S ECONOMY'S GONE UP IN SMOKE.

I.M.F.

The crowd that oversee the international financial system. In Fianna Fáil and Green Party circles, I.M.F. also stands for 'I'M F**ked'.

Income Stream

Any source of money. Ireland currently has a dried-up river bed.

THE MINISTER TODAY REFUTED CLAIMS THAT POOR BUSINESS INCOME STREAMS HAD LED TO A DOWNTURN IN THE BARBER SHOP INDUSTRY.

GOVERNMENT SPOKESMAN

NEWS

Information Architecture

Awful business blather that means the way information is organized.

BULLSHIT BOX

'The bank will be managing the balance sheet at year end.'
Willie McAteer, then Finance Director of Anglo Irish Bank

'Fair play to you, Willie!
Patrick Neary, then Chief Executive of the Financial Regulator

At a meeting on 24 September 2008, as reported in The Sunday Tribune, *22 February 2009.*

Interface *(see also Face Time)*

Yet more oul' guff meaning 'to have a meeting.'

Insource

Instead of paying someone else to do something, having to get off your arse and do it yourself.

Joined-up Thinking

Making all the elements work together to produce the best result. The nearest we have to this in

Ireland is 'Joined-up Drinking', when a gang of us get plastered while we moan about how banjaxed we are.

Light Touch Regulation

Unfortunately the Department of Finance thought this was a type of dimmer switch system you could buy in Woodies DIY. By the time they copped on, the economy had been thrown into the dark ages.

BULLSHIT BOX

'We are in a zone of financial stability in a very troubled financial world.'

Minister for Finance, Brian Lenihan, as reported in The Irish Times, *October 2009.*

Mainstreaming

Going with the flow.
The recommended response to an individual using this term in a

sentence is to give said individual a root in the arse.

Meat and Potatoes Approach

Getting back to the basics as a way of solving the country's economic woes. The term is generally used by muttonheads and turnips.

WHAT WE NEED SEAN, IS A MEAT AND POTATOES APPROACH TO IRELAND'S PROBLEMS.

I AGREE. YES WAITER I'LL HAVE THE CAVIAR FOLLOWED BY THE PHEASANT MARINATED IN VINTAGE CHAMPAGNE

NAMA

Acronym for National Asset
Management Agency
(See explanatory diagram)

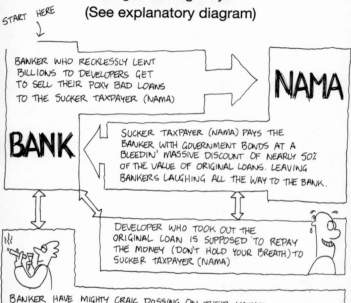

START HERE ↓

BANKER WHO RECKLESSLY LENT
BILLIONS TO DEVELOPERS GET
TO SELL THEIR POXY BAD LOANS
TO THE SUCKER TAXPAYER (NAMA)

NAMA

BANK

SUCKER TAXPAYER (NAMA) PAYS THE
BANKER WITH GOVERNMENT BONDS AT A
BLEEDIN' MASSIVE DISCOUNT OF NEARLY 50%
OF THE VALUE OF ORIGINAL LOANS. LEAVING
BANKERS LAUGHING ALL THE WAY TO THE BANK.

DEVELOPER WHO TOOK OUT THE
ORIGINAL LOAN IS SUPPOSED TO REPAY
THE MONEY (DON'T HOLD YOUR BREATH) TO
SUCKER TAXPAYER (NAMA)

BANKER HAVE MIGHTY CRAIC DOSSING ON THEIR YACHTS,
GUZZLING CHAMPAGNE, TAKING THEIR PRIVATE JETS TO BARBADOS,
WHILE YOU WORK YOUR ARSE OFF TO TRY AND PAY BACK ALL THE
MONEY THEY FLUSHED DOWN THE JACKS.

Outsource

In business terms, the word
'outsource' scares the shite out of
workers as it is usually followed

soon after by the words 'you're fired.' Their work is then done by some desperately poor fecker in a sweatshop in Thailand.

YES, YES MR O'MEARA, I KNOW YOU'VE BEEN A LOYAL EMPLOYEE FOR OVER 20 YEARS AND ARE HIGHLY SKILLED, BUT ARE YOU PREPARED TO WORK A 15-HOUR DAY FOR 80 CENTS AN HOUR?

GLOBAL GEEBAG INC.

Pension

Ginormous sum of money paid by a bank or government to individual for making a complete bollix of something.

€1,000,000

YIPEEE! FREE MONEY

Prevailing Philosophy

Jargon meaning 'current thinking'. The actual prevailing philosophy among ordinary Irish people regarding government bullshit about economic recovery is the one expounded by the Greek philosopher Pyrrho around 300 BC. It's called 'Skepticism.'

HMM, YES, THE PREVAILING PHILOSOPHY AMONG DENTISTS IS TO MAINTAIN OUR EXORBITANT PROFIT LEVELS BY CUTTING BACK ON ANASTHETIC...

Property Bubble

Dodgy planning officials, money-grabbing bankers, narcissistic property developers. With so many little pricks around, the bubble was bound to burst.

Protectionism

In most countries this means protecting trade by putting tariffs on imports etc, but in Ireland it refers to the policy in high places of protecting your rich, crooked cronies from losing their money or being thrown in the slammer for dodgy business dealings.

Rationalization

You're either getting the boot or are expected to break your bollix for more hours and less pay.

MY MISTRESS WANTS DIAMONDS THAT COST €50K. YOUR SALARY IS €50K. IF I FIRE YOU AND GET THE OTHERS TO WORK HARDER, IT DOESN'T COST ME A CENT AND I CAN STILL GET LAID BY A 20 YEAR-OLD NYMPHO NOW THATS WHAT I CALL RATIONALISATION.

Readjustments

You're fired.

Recession

Period from September 2008 to day Ireland win the World Cup.

Redundant

Term frequently used to describe
the Government.

Rightsizing

Jargon for firing just the right number of unfortunate head-the-balls so that none of the directors have to take a pay cut.

Road Mapping
(See also Horizon Scanning)

Blather that means 'planning for a company's or a country's future.' As our road mapping in the past has driven us over a cliff, a lot of

companies are taking the route
straight out of Ireland.

Sharing the Pain

Term used by government to
explain why we must all share the
burden to get ourselves out of the
mess they put us in.
See pie chart below for distribution
of shared economic pain.

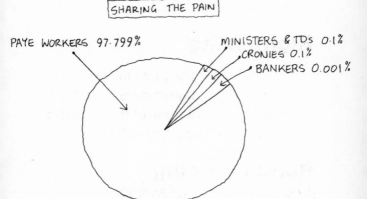

SHARING THE PAIN

PAYE WORKERS 97.799%

MINISTERS & TDs 0.1%
CRONIES 0.1%
BANKERS 0.001%

Slayoff

The way some employers fire
people: by locking company doors

and leaving a note on the outside, by leaving a message on the employee's voicemail, leaving a note on his/her chair or sending a mass company e-mail. Don't you have to have a father before you can be an employer?

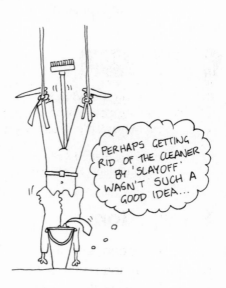

Social Partnership

In theory, getting everyone to make sacrifices for a better Ireland. ('Everyone' in this context excludes

TDs, members of the Golden Circle, certain senior public servants, political cronies, many senior banking executives, a large number of property developers and various other buddies who dine/drink in a variety of Kildare Street establishments.)

BULLSHIT BOX

'If I was to give advice to people, I would say, go out and buy some property now. It's great value.'

Frank Fahey, Fianna Fáil TD
Irish Independent, *15 March 2008*.

Staycation

American term that has crept in here meaning 'thanks to the recession I'm too bleedin' broke for a holiday so I'm spending my two weeks arsing around my house doing feck all.'

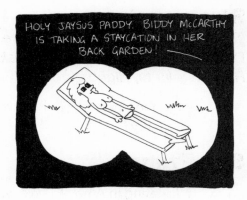

Stimulus Package

Various economic measures, like tax incentives or grants to projects, to try and kick-start the Irish economy. Sort of like giving Viagra to a eunuch.

BULLSHIT BOX

'Irish banks are resilient and have good shock absorption capacity to cope with the current situation.'

Patrick Neary, former Chief Executive of the Financial Regulator, 19 September 2008.

Streamlining

(See also Cost Reduction Initiative, Decruitment, Downsizing, Rationalizing, Readjustments, Rightsizing)

Jargon for 'here's your hat, what's your hurry?'

Sub Prime

Originating in America, this was the stupid practice of lending huge sums of money to buy vastly over-priced houses to poor eejits who hadn't a snowball's chance in hell of repaying the loan. Became a model for Irish economic thinking for years.

YOU ONLY EARN €40K? PERFECT! HERE'S YOUR CHANCE TO LIVE THE AMERICAN DREAM RIGHT HERE IN BALLYDEHOB!

FOR SALE ONE BED COTTAGE ONLY €2,000,000

Synergies

Teamwork. Why in the name of Jaysus can't they just say teamwork??!!

Too big to fail

When an institution has its grubby little fingers in so many financial pies that if it collapses lots of cute hoors might have to be arrested and thrown in the slammer, it is officially deemed 'too big to fail'.

We are where we are

This has become the popular way with bankers, developers and politicians of saying: 'No use crying over spilt milk (i.e. about €50 Billion), let's wipe the slate clean and get out of this mess (that they put us in).' Yes, we are where we are, but you're not where you should be.

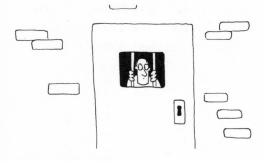

BULLSHIT BOX

'Property still looks like providing fantastic opportunities in the years ahead.'

Marian Finnegan, Chief Economist for Sherry Fitzgerald, The Irish Independent, 13 January 2006.

Worklessness

The condition of doing nothing from one end of the week to the other, much like the Cabinet during the 'boom' era.

Zombie Bank

A financial institution that has a net worth less than zero but continues to operate because its gurrier executives have been promised credit in the form of taxpayers' money. Appropriately, Zombie Banks are the main reason we have Ghost Estates.

...YEAH, EVERYONE IN NIGERIA IS GETTING E-MAILS FROM THE BANKS BEGGING THEM TO INVEST MONEY IN IRELAND.

WHAT A SCAM.

BOUT THE BOOK OF IRISH SONGS YER

HOOLEY THE FECKIN' BOOK OF IRISH S

THE BOOK OF LUVELY IRISH RECIPES

RIER THE FECKIN' BOOK OF IRISH SAYI

WER OF SAVAGES THE 2ND FECKIN' BOO

FIRST ONE THE FECKIN' BOOK OF IRISH

HALF AS USEFUL THE BOOK OF FECK

RS AND BOWSIES THE BOOK OF DEADLY

IS ALWAYS BLATHERIN' ON ABOUT THE

WHEN HE WAS JARRED AT A HOOLEY TH

OR DACENT PEOPLE'S EYES THE BOOK

YOU WERE A LITTLE GURRIER THE FEC

HE BATTER WITH A SHOWER OF SAVAG

ES A HOLY SHOW OF THE FIRST ONE TH

HICK AS MANURE AND ONLY HALF AS US

T CRAIC FOR CUTE HOORS AND BOWSIE

T FECKER IN THE PUB IS ALWAYS BLAT

FELLA ALWAYS SANG WHEN HE WAS JA

LOVE THAT'S NOT FIT FOR DACENT PEO

MA USETA MAKE WHEN YOU WERE A LITT

WHEN YOU GO ON THE BATTER WITH A

SLANG THAT MAKES A HOLY SHOW

TS FOR GOBDAWS AS THICK AS MAN